Look
BEYOND
the Obvious

Look BEYOND *the Obvious*

A BLUEPRINT FOR
Transforming Managers into Leaders

EDWARD F. SCHULTZ

Copyright © 2016 Edward F. Schultz.

All rights reserved. No part of this book may be used or reproduced by any means, graphic, electronic, or mechanical, including photocopying, recording, taping or by any information storage retrieval system without the written permission of the author except in the case of brief quotations embodied in critical articles and reviews.

Archway Publishing books may be ordered through booksellers or by contacting:

Archway Publishing
1663 Liberty Drive
Bloomington, IN 47403
www.archwaypublishing.com
1 (888) 242-5904

Because of the dynamic nature of the Internet, any web addresses or links contained in this book may have changed since publication and may no longer be valid. The views expressed in this work are solely those of the author and do not necessarily reflect the views of the publisher, and the publisher hereby disclaims any responsibility for them.

Any people depicted in stock imagery provided by Thinkstock are models, and such images are being used for illustrative purposes only. Certain stock imagery © Thinkstock.

ISBN: 978-1-4808-2178-1 (sc)
ISBN: 978-1-4808-2179-8 (hc)
ISBN: 978-1-4808-2180-4 (e)

Library of Congress Control Number: 2015916511

Print information available on the last page.

Archway Publishing rev. date: 5/3/2016

CEO'S RAISON D'ÊTRE

THE CUSTOMER

- ♪ To understand that it's the customer who pays the bills.
- ♪ To empathize and see your business through your customer's eyes.
- ♪ To recognize that creating and retaining customers is the business.

BUSINESS PRINCIPLES

- ♪ To increase revenue and growth, but to do it profitably!
- ♪ To partner with attitudes *not* credentials.
- ♪ To define responsibilities, authority, and empowerment at all levels.
- ♪ To never employ the Peter Principle for anyone or anything.
- ♪ To ensure continuous education and training at all levels.
- ♪ To utilize project management as a strategic weapon.
- ♪ To be aware of the consequences of management indecision.
- ♪ To realize in business that everything is a performance issue.
- ♪ To understand and practice the Five Laws of Business religiously.

LEADERSHIP PRINCIPLES

- To recognize that luck is preparation meeting opportunity and is always an unstoppable force when driven by the proper attitude.
- To never allow yourself to get married to a business idea.
- To remember that listening is the other half of communication.
- To practice the art of MBWA (management by walking around), rather than the science of illusion.
- To know tomorrow is important, but today is critical to your success.
- To set your goals and objectives just out of reach, but not out of sight.
- To work on the correct things rather than the important things.
- To be aware of new technology and how it will affect your future.
- To demand simple strategies to resolve problems, questions, issues, and concerns.
- To lead, encourage, and motivate with rewards and recognition.
- To resolve internal conflicts respectfully and immediately!
- To always lead from the front and expect the best!
- To begin each day knowing *war* in business means …

We are ready!

CONTENTS

FOREWORD XI

PART 1: The Customer

INSIGHT 1 3
To understand that it's the customer who pays the bills.

INSIGHT 2 11
To empathize and see your business through your customer's eyes.

INSIGHT 3 19
To recognize that creating and retaining customers is the business.

PART 2: Business Principles

INSIGHT 1 27
To increase revenue and growth, but to do it profitably!

INSIGHT 2 .... **31**
To partner with attitudes not credentials.

INSIGHT 3 .... **35**
To define responsibilities, authority,
and empowerment at all levels.

INSIGHT 4 .... **37**
To never employ the Peter Principle for anyone or anything.

INSIGHT 5 .... **39**
To ensure continuous education and training at all levels.

INSIGHT 6 .... **43**
To utilize project management as a strategic weapon.

INSIGHT 7 .... **49**
To be aware of the consequences of management indecision.

INSIGHT 8 .... **53**
To realize in business that everything is a performance issue.

INSIGHT 9 .... **57**
To understand and practice the Five
Laws of Business religiously.

PART 3: Leadership Principles

INSIGHT 1 .... **63**
To recognize that luck is preparation meeting
opportunity and is always an unstoppable
force when driven by the proper attitude.

INSIGHT 2 .... **69**
To never allow yourself to get married to a business idea.

INSIGHT 3 73
*To remember that listening is the other
half of communication.*

INSIGHT 4 77
*To practice the art of MBWA (management by walking
around), rather than the science of illusion.*

INSIGHT 5 81
*To know tomorrow is important, but
today is critical to your success.*

INSIGHT 6 87
*To set your goals and objectives just out
of reach, but not out of sight.*

INSIGHT 7 91
*To work on the correct things rather
than the important things.*

INSIGHT 8 95
*To be aware of new technology and
how it will affect your future.*

INSIGHT 9 99
*To demand simple strategies to resolve
problems, questions, issues, and concerns.*

INSIGHT 10 105
*To lead, encourage, and motivate with
rewards and recognition.*

INSIGHT 11 109
To resolve internal conflicts respectfully and immediately!

INSIGHT 12 113
To always lead from the front and expect the best!

INSIGHT 13 .... **117**
*To begin each day knowing war in
business means ... We are ready!*

EPILOGUE **121**
Is America Looking Beyond the Obvious?

SEVEN RULES FOR BUSINESS SUCCESS **133**

FOREWORD

Throughout the ages, it's the visionary or dreamer who sets the stage for the next technological breakthrough and their resulting benefits to mankind. It's the visionary or dreamer who provides the technological foundation for history's unprecedented resulting lifestyles.

Here's an old economics question: How many people does it take to make a pair of shoes? Well, let's start with the producer of the ultimate raw material—the farmer.

The farmer provides the leather, but first you need cattle. So you buy cattle, and then you have to feed and care for them. Where does the food come from and how did it get there? Where did the shelter come from? How was it made and from what? Who built the shelter and with what tools and equipment? Where did the tools and equipment come from?

Later, the transportation of the leather means cars, trucks, trains, planes, ships, and the employees involved in the manufacture and transportation of those goods and services. Where did the steel to build those cars, trucks, trains, planes, and ships come from? How many people—engineers, metallurgists, steelworkers, and so on—in the mill did it take to make the steel? You can go on and on, but I think you get the point. It's a lot of people!

So let's look at technological breakthroughs from a different viewpoint. How many jobs did Thomas Edison create? Andrew Carnegie? Henry Ford? How many innovations came from these simple start-ups? How many businesses supporting these businesses were created? These visionaries or dreamers all had at least one thing in common: They acted on their vision, started the business, and at the end of the day had created an industry. These are also some of the greatest examples of successful entrepreneurship.

This was all possible because these visionaries simply took a chance. Taking risks and going for it is truly the American way. They rolled the dice, risked it all, and won big time! Did they make any money for their efforts? Absolutely, but their guiding principle was not profit for the sake of profit. Their prime directive may have been to make money or enhance society, build their business or whatever, but before that could happen, they needed to keep the front doors open. They understood this simple concept especially in those early years:

Revenue minus Expenses = What?

Owners and CEOs need to focus on what makes their organization run like a finely tuned performance racing engine. The CEO's sole responsibility is to lead the organization, acquire new business, and increase revenue, growth, and profitability. Naturally, as the entrepreneur in the start-up phase, you performed all manners of glorious tasks within the organization, including mowing the lawn, mopping the floors, removing the trash, and cleaning the bathrooms. I can relate, as I grew up in a family business and was intimately familiar with all these tasks. My life revolved around mopping, sweeping, and loading and unloading trucks until I was around twelve. My father called these character-building exercises. I had a different interpretation.

As your business grew, you had to decide whether or not to remain the technical expert or to focus on management of the business. Few individuals can perform both at the highest levels. If you think you are in that rarified air of performing both functions at the highest levels then …

You can stop right here! You obviously do not need to continue.

However, if you think you may have room to improve or may learn something new, you may want to continue and *look beyond the obvious.*

This book is composed of three parts—The Customer, Business Principles, and Leadership Principles—containing twenty-five insights based on my experiences in manufacturing and business.

Please consider these insights in your journey. I wish you the best in your future endeavors.

PART 1
The Customer

INSIGHT 1

To understand that it's the customer who pays the bills.

True leaders know the difference between *leadership* and *management*. Some say experience is a great teacher, and it is. But if you have negative experiences, it's tough to gain a positive perspective on leadership and management.

How much and what kind of experience is beneficial? Only you can truly determine the answer to that.

I have made more mistakes than I care to remember, but I learned to always get up, brush myself off, and forge ahead. Do that enough times and you tend to quickly become knowledgeable, skilled, and experienced. People notice that you anticipate situations, bring value to the discussion, and have a different way of looking at things. Coworkers may think you are smart, and you may be, but your immediate manager or supervisor, in all probability, may see you as a threat. In the beginning, mine always did.

Just remember that self-preservation—or CYA (cover your ass)—is always present and should be studiously considered in any analysis of your situation.

The true leader encourages, mentors, and promotes you and your ideas. If that is not happening, you may be working with a manager or supervisor—not a leader—and that can be career ending if you allow it to continue. Once you have determined this reality, start looking for a new position immediately. Don't waste precious time trying to remake the manager or supervisor into a leader. It doesn't work! I know. I have tried way too many times, thinking I was actually helping.

The business world has enough managers and supervisors. What is desperately needed in business are leaders. Leaders, who know how to lead, are technically competent, and who know how to get things done, work with and through people, and have the vision to inspire greatness. These attributes are a rare commodity.

In my case, reality actually knocked on my door one day. It didn't exactly become that obvious to me or happen overnight. It was a combination of what I was taught, learned, thought I had learned, and studied as I started on a lifelong journey through a business and manufacturing obstacle course. This obstacle course revealed the reality of what I actually learned, thought I had learned, experienced, and eventually figured out for myself. The lessons gleaned from questioning the status quo and its logical conclusions always proved true long after the hype of the latest product release, the game of the week, or the program of the month fizzled out.

Here is an interesting question for you:

Revenue minus Expenses = What?

Think you know the answer and what it represents? Good for you!

But just so you know, the answer is not "profit."

Try again.

The answer actually goes far beyond just profit, although profit in business is the name of the game. Your revenue, growth, and profitability must be in balance, and therein lays the secret to your success. Understand this:

> You cannot plan your way to your strategy, nor can you spend your way to a sustainable success.

Revenue minus expenses fundamentally equals your future. Think about it. If you truly think you understand this simple expression, you are light-years ahead of the pack. Your career has fast-tracked you through the Harvard MBA program, saving one to three years of your life, a lot of work, and a considerable amount of money.

Good job!

For most, though, it's a long rise to the top. Some make it; some don't. If you really understand the expression above, you need to ask yourself if you are either that good or have been just plain lucky in your career.

OBSERVATION

The concept of the relationship between business and the customer is relatively simple. You are in business to make money to pay yourself, your personnel, and your suppliers, as well as the lights, heat, insurance, office supplies, and materials, but it's actually the customer who pays the bills.

> You just write the checks.

As the founder, owner, chairman, CEO, or president of an enterprise, you know through experience that the vast majority of your employees have no idea how the organization functions, pays its bills, or looks ahead to ensure its continuing existence. Why should they? That's what they have been taught and are conditioned to think, directly and indirectly, since they started their career in this profession we call "working." They are there to simply work and get paid at the end of each week.

There is just one problem with this scenario. With the billions spent every year in marketing and advertising, how many times have you heard the experts contend that you can't forget the customer? But when we think in terms of an order, a product, service, or delivery, we just did forget the customer. Hundreds of books have been written on why customers are important and how we need to retain our employees. But too many employees seem to be totally disconnected from their customers and how their job affects the company's relationship with the customer.

In the ever-popular, half-day seminar, the customer is always sacrosanct above all else because the customer is the reason the business exists. It's absolutely true! However, that's all well and good in the seminar, but do your employees actually know and care that it's the customer who pays the bills and why that is important?

Ever heard salespeople say, "We got the job and that means I did my job. What else do you want me to do?" Don't you hear the birds chirping? Did you see the pot of gold at the end of the rainbow? Can you appreciate the blue skies without the fear of those troublesome black clouds or dark days materializing? Don't you feel better knowing all those things will work out because that's what you hoped for? Doesn't that just sound wonderful?

In my book, your job is just beginning. A handoff—or throwing the responsibility over the fence to engineering, manufacturing, or quality control—is simply an excuse to relieve oneself of responsibility as an advocate for the customer. The salesperson may not be directly involved or have any responsibility for the ultimate delivery, but the salesperson should be the one leading the advocacy for the customer.

Whether you and your employees realize it or not, every action and inaction impacts the customer and your continuing relationship. Do you and your team truly understand the significance of these relationships? If not, it's a failure on your part. In fact, at the end of the day, it's always a management problem, issue, question, or concern not identified or resolved. You need to educate and train your staff on these critical relationships.

Remember, as the leader of the organization, if it's not important to you as demonstrated by your actions or lack thereof, then why should it be important to anyone else on your staff?

I know, I know. You can't educate and train everybody because they leave and it costs too much. But here's the flip side of not educating and training everybody: retention.

What does it cost your enterprise for your employees to perform inefficiently or ineffectively on a daily basis? Apparently not enough for you to take corrective action. Through your inaction, aren't you broadcasting that you are expecting a different result? How's that working out for you?

Consider this:

Retention! Retention! Retention!

It's the least expensive, company-wide employee benefit imaginable. The cost of new hires and turnovers is considerable. Have you even bothered to calculate what it's costing the company in turnovers and ramping back up to acceptable productivity with new hires?

Unless circumstances dictate otherwise, make the effort to retain your personnel. Great employees are hard to find, even tougher to keep, and retaining them doesn't happen magically.

Think of it this way: Your least expensive sales are to current business customers. They are a known commodity, require low maintenance, have a quality reputation, and are reliable. Studies have shown it takes approximately five sales calls to produce that first order. It's the cost of doing business, of course, but when working with an existing customer, those costs have virtually disappeared, making each sale much more profitable.

With existing employees, don't you have a similar set of circumstances? Your employees are a known commodity, require low maintenance, have a quality reputation, and have proven to be reliable. Sounds more like you have made a quality investment to me.

Making that investment in your workforce always pays dividends.

Are you collecting those dividends or just paying your personnel for their cost of doing business as placeholders? My question to you is ...

> Do you have the right people in the right place at the right time to be a successful organization?

INSIGHT 2

To empathize and see your business through your customer's eyes.

I once made this statement to the president of a company: "You should always give the customer more than what they expect." She said, and I quote, "If you do that, we will all be looking for a job."

Of course, if taken literally, she was correct.

I explained that I was referring to customer service—specifically doing those things that the customer has not paid for directly but that would secure the next order and commitment to future sales. In other words, going beyond what the customer expected. For example, this can include

- answering the telephone before the third ring;
- promptly returning telephone calls;
- taking ownership of the customer's problem;

- resolving the customer's problem, issue, question, or concern; and
- Delivering on time.

ANSWERING THE TELEPHONE BEFORE THE THIRD RING

It's not terribly complicated, but all parties need to understand that the professional image they collectively project is far more important than the "someone else will get it" attitude that permeates some organizations.

PROMPTLY RETURNING TELEPHONE CALLS

No matter what business you are in, service is what sells. For that matter, all businesses are in the service business. I'll reiterate that again: no matter what the product or service, all businesses are in the service business.

There is nothing more irritating than waiting for someone to return a call within a reasonable amount of time. The solution is simple. Acknowledge the call and respond with a time when you will return the call, e-mail, and so on. The customer realizes you are busy but appreciates that you have established the receipt of the call and, more importantly, that the customer is critical to you and your organization.

TAKING OWNERSHIP OF THE CUSTOMER'S PROBLEM

A clothing store had a sale. Upon picking up the items we needed and several things we had to have, we approached the kiosk to pay the bill. After waiting approximately five minutes, we went to another kiosk and waited. Then we went to another department and asked for the store manager. The young lady inquired if she could be of assistance. I thanked her and said I simply wanted to point out something to the store manager that could help his operation. The young lady looked skeptical but made the call.

The store manager arrived within minutes and asked if there was a problem. I said, "No, but I may have a solution to a problem that you may not even be aware of." That got her attention!

We walked back to the first kiosk, and I proceeded to take a twenty-dollar bill out of my wallet and ask, "Is there anyone here who can take my money?"

Absolutely no response!

The store manager looked perplexed but didn't say anything immediately. Then a light bulb went on, and she got the point and paged for assistance. Another five to seven minutes of waiting.

Now the store manager was not perplexed anymore and finally said something really profound. "I'll be right back."

Another ten minutes passed, but it was well worth the wait.

Suddenly a beehive of activity erupted and personnel materialized from everywhere. The store manager apologized profusely and rang up the items at no charge. I said that wasn't necessary, but she insisted.

As we left, I noticed every kiosk was staffed. Amazing how that works. Now that's action-oriented problem solving, even if it was after the fact.

This situation demonstrates that not only was the store manager not aware of any opportunities for improvement, but she wasn't even aware there was a problem! More importantly, by not addressing this dysfunctional operation, what was the message to staff? That's right. "This is acceptable behavior and/or how we conduct our daily business." What a message!

DELIVERING ON TIME

The product was not finished and delivered until Tuesday of the following week rather than on Friday of the previous week as originally promised. As a consequence, the customer's employees were sent home.

I asked the group if they should be sent home next time one of their suppliers did not deliver on time. They got the message.

As they say in the game of pool, "There is a lot of green between here and there," regarding the preparation and execution of the winning shot. The same could be said of the sales process. In quality speak, the drivers are quality, cost, and delivery, but these must remain flexible enough to achieve maximum agility.

For example, the customers notify you of their intention to purchase a product or service from your organization. They want your product or service based on your reputation (that's the quality part), they have already agreed to the price (that's the cost part), and they have agreed to your delivery (obviously that's the delivery part).

From the customers' viewpoint, the only thing they can't control is your delivery. And guess what the issue becomes when you are late?

That right! Your value to their organization!

Any savings projected or future business relationships may now be in jeopardy because of your lack of understanding or the outright ambivalence throughout your organization, regarding the word *delivery* and its meaning to the customers. The customers aren't interested in the price anymore. They are not interested in the quality prior to receiving their shipment. They are only interested in their delivery.

> Delivery! Delivery! Delivery! = Performance

OBSERVATION

As the leader of a company, we work with and through people. Once you hire people to grow your business, you had better understand that the days of you being able to accomplish everything to your personal standards are history. You hired people to take on and accomplish the work that you could not accomplish single-handedly anymore.

Pundits speak of people being a company's greatest asset, but many companies fail to realize the benefits of having staff working at 110 percent rather than at 80 percent of capacity because of the self-imposed limitations, rules, and regulations we place on those greatest assets.

Pundits generally say a lot but seldom have the practical knowledge and experience of the seasoned owner. Pundits remind me of the arm-chair quarterback: phenomenal strategic knowledge and skills on paper in the classroom or in the family room on Sunday watching the game, but not on the field or in a real business situation with their own money at risk. Generally they are not as phenomenal as they think, and they are usually wrong.

In my experience, the company's foundation of revenue, growth, and profitability is going no further than the average level of its personnel's knowledge, skills, and experience.

Your job is to continually raise the level of that foundation and resolve the customer's problem, issue, question, or concern to create a win-win situation.

Don't ever forget this!

You may be surprised how many companies have actual distain for their customers' problems. "They're too busy." "They don't give us enough work" or whatever. This strategic assessment and historical attitude may work in the short term, but if you start losing customers, you need only look in the mirror to get the answer.

It's more than just shipping a product or providing a service.

> It's your reputation, and your reputation is your livelihood.

INSIGHT 3

To recognize that creating and retaining customers is the business.

As the owner, CEO or president of a company, your only business is the business.

This should be your focus every single day of your professional life. If you provide a quality product or service at a competitive price and deliver on time all the time, you'll be in a profitable business for many years to come, no matter what the economic climate.

Many times I have sat in management meetings only to be amazed with the continual emphasis on the financials, i.e., the P&L (profit and loss statement). These are historical facts and represent all of the management decisions and indecisions during a designated time period. Bad practice equals bad results. Unless you correct the practices, the results will continue to be bad.

In many cases top management doesn't understand that the vast majority of management teams below the Fortune 1000 have neither the college-level financial education nor the accounting skills to interpret the data presented. The emphasis should be on financial management, i.e., solving the immediate and systemic problems to achieve positive results.

Are the financials important? Absolutely. But not at the expense of the company's personnel who may not see the connection between decision, indecision, and results, and its impact on them and/or your operation. Think of it this way: Accounting is the history, and financial management is the future. The question should be "How can we translate the results of our historical actions into positive successful results in the future?"

What if the president says one thing but means something completely different, and no one is the wiser as to the president's real intentions? Don't misunderstand; management decisions should be based on the information that the data and/or statistical evidence represent because you cannot manage what you don't know. By that I mean, why the president states "We need to be more productive and make more money" is sometimes less important than how those statements are delivered! Increasing revenue alone or cutting expenses may not be in the long-term best interests of the company if the purpose of the directive is not explained thoroughly and received positively. If presented in a questionable manner, these statements may be misinterpreted by the employees.

Typically, these types of leaders don't last long because they are truly only interested in themselves and most likely not interested in the company, its employees, or its customers. I have seen that slice of corporate America ruin lives, families, and companies all for personal gain far too many times. The wake begins as a ripple, but the total accumulation of these ripples creates waves of destruction and can almost never be repaired. It has bankrupted many long-standing but totally unsuspecting companies.

Worst-case scenario, these leaders may either be trying to justify their salary, trying to keep their job, or trying to maximize their bonus, thus keeping their job and justifying their salary at the expense of the employees and the company. Some are not so subtle in their delivery. If this occurs, you need to consider if you are in fact in the wrong place, need to survey the landscape, and perhaps move fast!

You probably have your own examples, but let's see if this profile hits the mark. The new president is presumably knowledgeable in everything managerial and technical. Of course that's how he or she got the job: the rising star, working his or her way to the top, being in the right place at the right time. Sounds good, the American dream.

Impressive!

But when you are only interested in preserving the status quo, hiring and firing personnel to look important, and continuing the same game plan so you can sail into retirement (which is what you are actually working toward), how does this help the customers, the employees, and the continuation of the business? It won't. It will not add any value now or in the future. Self-aggrandizing, risk-adverse policies and procedures are destructive in the long run.

Of course, this illusion may continue to work for some time, especially in good economies or through specialization, but when either or both are affected by an economic downturn or unsustainability, they have nothing of substance to offer. During this time frame, how many customers could have been added? How much revenue and growth could have been achieved had they not chosen to save money by reducing expenses for expense sake?

Did you get the facts or did you just make your decision on what sounds good?

> When you start believing your own hype,
> you are well on your way to failure.

OBSERVATION

There is more to decision making than solely relying on data. Data can point you in a direction, but it should never be the only reason for developing a strategy.

Words like brainstorming, thinking outside the box, creative or critical thinking, or as I like to say, looking beyond the obvious become the spark or double-checks for reality. Will the products and services you have today keep you in business tomorrow? Next year? How about in three years?

When looking beyond the obvious isn't part of the discussion, it may be bad news on its way to happening for the home team. For example, if money is the end game, you may make money today, but what about tomorrow? It's "in creditable" how easy and great it sounds on paper to reduce expenses. The always-popular quick fix eliminates long-term employees, cuts back on benefits and pensions, and so on. But did you realize during your strategic epiphany that you just let your expertise walk right out the door into the open arms of your competitors or potential competitors?

I know, I know, they didn't have a college degree, and they obviously don't have the knowledge, skills, and/or actually know anything. They just started and built the company over the past thirty years. Why would they know anything about the business?

Think about this: Are you really more secure today in your own situation than you were yesterday? If you are fighting upstream in the wake of self-indulgence, your career and/or your business are slowly sinking. It may be a good time to plug the holes, put on the life vest, and/or abandon ship before it's too late.

> Personally and professionally, if you can't understand why you are not successful in your career or are not making the revenue, growth, and profitability you expect as a business, you can't BS the person in the mirror.

PART 2
Business Principles

INSIGHT 1

To increase revenue and growth, but to do it profitably!

The CEO said to the assembled group, "We need to increase sales. Any ideas?"

"Yes," I said. "I can double your sales by the end of the day."

Management's response was predictable and ranged from outright snickering to polite sarcasm. However, I was serious and repeated my statement, this time saying each word slowly for emphasis to maximize attention.

The CEO said, "Prove it!"

"If I can have the names of your top ten customers and their telephone numbers, I will call them and make them an offer that will sound so unbelievable; it will be too good to pass up. Believe me, they won't."

The CEO said, "That's terrific! Just how do you plan on doing that?"

"I will tell each of your customers that because of their unique relationship with us over the years and their continued loyalty, they are the recipients of a fantastic once-in-a-lifetime deal. During the next three days, they can purchase any of our products or services in any quantity for fifty percent off our standard pricing. We will even pay the shipping. No strings. No BS!"

It was pretty quiet for the next few seconds. I said, "Is there anyone here who would like to disagree and place a bet that your customers will not take advantage of this offer? Remember the premise: we need to increase sales."

"We won't make any money!" the CEO said frantically.

"You certainly will if your goal was to simply increase sales. How can you not have an increase in sales when you will have more sales tomorrow than you did the day before?"

The CEO said, "I get it. Yes, we could certainly do this, but you can't do this profitably, which is your point."

OBSERVATION

In order to be successful in business, you must generate the revenue necessary to sustain operations, continue to grow your products and services, and do these profitably. A growth strategy that does not consider revenue and profitability and its counterpart, cash flow, is not sustainable. You can break even, but you may not grow. You can be extremely profitable, but you may not necessarily grow. The combinations are endless.

So here's the problem: If you don't grow and are not profitable, you may not be able to control your own destiny. You need to decide if you want to maintain a smaller business or grow to capitalize on new opportunities and technology.

Revenue, growth, and profitability are not economic islands; they must work together. Don't make the mistake of focusing on one at the expense of the other two. Make sure you have your business foundation in place, which is the capacity required to deliver the correct combination of what I call a balanced approach to revenue, growth, and profitability: the knowledge, skills, and strategic and risk management capabilities to capitalize on your initiatives.

Here are some questions to consider:

1. Do you have the capacity to deliver?

2. Are your functional areas prepared to take on additional sales and commitments?

3. Do you have the necessary cash flow to support these new sales?

4. What if the sales don't materialize? What's Plan B?

Now consider this mini-strategic plan from the one-hundred-thousand-foot level:

1. Where are you today?

2. Where do you want to be tomorrow? Why?

3. How are you going to get there?

Increasing sales is the easiest thing in the world to accomplish. Everyone loves a deal. Free or something close to it will always bring new interest, new customers, and new sales, but at what cost?

What else can you do for your customers? Look at your current clientele and see if other sales opportunities are available. Your manufacturing equipment doesn't know or care what it is producing ... why do you?

It's amazing how many customers may not be aware of your total capabilities. Don't assume your customers are up to speed.

> Ask your customers how you can
> help them achieve their goals!

INSIGHT 2

To partner with attitudes not credentials.

Years ago when I was applying for a machinist / tool and die position, I sat down with the model shop supervisor for my job interview. After about two minutes, he said, "Why should I hire you? You have no experience, and I don't need another nineteen-year-old tool and die maker with your self-inflated twenty years of experience."

I said, "Are you willing to take on someone who is willing to learn?"

"What do you mean?"

"I will work for you for the next week so you can make an assessment of my capabilities, strengths, and weaknesses. If I don't measure up to your expectations, we go our separate ways at no charge. Fair enough?"

He asked when I could start. That's how I got my first job!

Under his supervision, I was operating milling machines and lathes and asking a lot of questions. On Friday of that first week, the entire model shop (engineers, tool and die makers, and machinists) gathered around to announce that I had made the cut and welcomed me aboard.

I even got a raise!

OBSERVATION

At the time, I wasn't even thinking they actually had to pay me for my limited services, but the offer was made with good intentions, and it became the foundation of my **Bold Innovative Moves Strategy,** or simply stated, thinking outside my imaginary box.

If I thought I could do it, I made every effort to achieve it. If I discovered my projected goal would never materialize, I just looked at how far I had come and capitalized on the knowledge, skills, and experience I had gained in the effort and said, "Next." A whole new world had opened before my eyes, one that started me on this journey through business, engineering, and manufacturing. I discovered the value of continual improvement. Each day I became more valuable to my employer and later to my clients.

Continual improvement doesn't end at work. Learning doesn't end with high school or college. Become a lifelong learner. Think like a shark. A shark can never stop moving forward because water must pass through its gills to get oxygen. In order to grow and prosper, think like a shark.

In today's workplace, while you must never stop learning, always take care of yourself first. It pays dividends in ways that aren't always immediately apparent but are always relevant and marketable in the future. That's how you prosper and live longer.

The only limits we have are the ones we accept.

Don't stop moving forward!

OBSERVATION

During my daily tour through the facility, I came across a machinist looking at the information I had posted the day before. The posting listed by category our monthly costs of doing business for manufacturing, including the following items:

1. Setup
2. Productivity
3. Overtime

The machinist asked, "What does all this mean?"

Instead of giving him the standard math behind the posting, I changed the words and tried to make it more relevant.

"These initial costs-of-doing-business postings totaled approximately thirty-nine thousand dollars for the previous month, which included all twenty-eight categories."

He said, "That's a lot of money!"

Now came the fun part.

"Are you on the profit-sharing program?"

"Yes I am."

"Super! Let's go to the bank and withdraw thirty-nine thousand one-dollar bills. Then we will go out to the intersection and distribute a one-dollar bill to each car that passes by this afternoon. It's a main street, so we should be able to get rid of all this cash easily."

"Why would I do that?"

"This is precisely what you are doing every month these expenses are not addressed and resolved. You are quite literally just giving your profit sharing away! It's your money, so it's your choice."

I never spoke a word about this to anyone and never held a meeting to present these findings, but the next month's total was 42 percent below the previous month. What was even more interesting, the following month it dropped again and continued on a steady decline for some time.

> It's amazing what happens when common sense turns the lights on.

INSIGHT 3

To define responsibilities, authority, and empowerment at all levels.

I ordered a blue butterfly which arrived in a presentation case as a gift. Upon opening the package, I discovered the mounted butterfly was occupying the bottom of the presentation case.

Not good!

I was on the phone and explaining the situation when it occurred to me that the young lady was actually very interested in my dilemma. This customer service representative explained that the company would send a return label and appropriate return paperwork, and that I would have the replacement within five days.

I said, "Today is Tuesday and I need this by Thursday."

Without skipping a beat or asking her manager or supervisor, she said, "We will ship it to you overnight at no charge. I'll send you the return paperwork, and you can just send us the defective product when you get a chance."

Wow!

The gift arrived the next day in perfect condition.

OBSERVATION

I wrote a letter to the company and in part recommended the customer service representative should be considered for a raise. She was an outstanding reflection of the company's philosophy put into practice. Talk about empowerment! How refreshing.

> How does your customer service compare?

INSIGHT 4

To never employ the Peter Principle for anyone or anything.

This is and always will have the makings of a disaster on its way to happening. You got your start-up off the ground with capital from your uncle, who now expects his son or daughter to have a job for life with your new enterprise. Of course, the money from Mom helped, and magically your brother and sister now need jobs too.

The scenarios are endless. You may wind up paying for these potential placeholders or no-shows for a long time because of a mistake in judgment when you overran your headlights in your quest to get started.

Your education on operations and running a business successfully increased considerably since those early days because you learned the hard way that actions and inactions have consequences. At some point, you began to realize the full impact of what happened and how much you are paying for those apparent lapses in judgment now.

Right?

Now you see why you're uncomfortable and can't sleep. You are paying the price, and paying dearly, for decisions made in haste or desperation.

In a perfect world, you would not accept that premise because you realize that it is impossible to fulfill everyone's expectations. It is seldom that simple with family dynamics, but there are family businesses that are not plagued by the usual antics of family, in-laws, or *out*laws and function quite well, becoming the exception rather than the rule. Although rare, I have seen examples.

OBSERVATION

For those who haven't experienced the agony of trying to rationalize an irrational situation, my best advice is this: Don't go down that path unless you are personally and totally competent, are a skilled negotiator, and have the world's greatest relationships with your family of in-laws and outlaws. Otherwise, good luck!

> They say the devil is in the details, but if you really want to learn to dance, don't do it with the devil.

INSIGHT 5

To ensure continuous education and training at all levels.

During a meeting with a client, the discussion turned to flowcharts. I asked the vice president if the company had ever created a flowchart of their operation to identify any gaps, redundancies, and so on.

"Why yes," he said proudly. "Everyone in this company has been through classes on process management and flowcharting. In fact, all employees had a great deal of input into this flowchart." From a bookshelf he produced a voluminous book that was the compilation of their process management and flowcharting exercise. "Here, take a look at this and tell me what you think."

It was definitely big and expensively printed with detailed notes. On the first page, I noticed something odd. This particular flowchart began with receipt of the purchase order and continued through data entry, production control, scheduling, manufacturing, quality, and delivery. It was very impressive.

"So what happens when you don't get the order?" I asked.

He said, "What do you mean?"

"Don't you want to know why didn't get the order?"

He said it didn't matter.

Well, it does matter. You have time, money, and people invested in the sales call(s), securing the RFQ (request for quotation), and the actual sale. You cannot win them all, but if you are not closing as many deals as you think you should, doesn't that warrant further investigation?

I asked, "What trends can you identify? What are you doing right? What are you doing wrong? What opportunities could we capitalize on by simply getting what might be called traditional and nontraditional information? Do we need additional tools in our toolbox to raise the percentage of winning more bids, contracts, etcetera, in securing work?"

A young lady at the end of the conference table suddenly said, "I have been here nineteen years and I have never seen this book." Absolute dead silence permeated the conference room. Apparently, *everyone* only meant management. Not a good sign.

If not addressing new opportunities and/or your failures doesn't matter, what does?

OBSERVATION

The company is going no further than the average level of education and training, knowledge, expertise, skills, and the attitude of its employees. Even without turnover, education and training is quite often thought of as an expense rather than an investment. What better way to maximize your efficiency and effectiveness than to upgrade the knowledge, skills, and expertise of your workforce?

Education and training via high school or college is only the entry card to gaining employment because it demonstrates your character, discipline, and perseverance. Continual education and training is necessary just to keep up and keep you employed.

Think of training as learning the steps or instructions required to execute a task or process. Education then is developing and applying your knowledge, skills, expertise, and attitude to maximize the execution of the task or process efficiently and effectively.

Granted, you are not in the education and training business as a product or service, but most people would agree that if you can't know everything or have the expertise necessary to conduct business efficiently and effectively, you need additional people.

Education is like breathing; it never stops for those who have the knowledge, skills, and attitude to continually learn and move themselves and their business forward, no matter what their age. Just remember …

> Training people is the inverse of educating dogs.
> You train dogs, but you educate people!

INSIGHT 6

To utilize project management as a strategic weapon.

Each and every business has the same three resources: time, money, and people. The fundamental differences among businesses are how they conduct business on a daily basis, how much money they earn, and how many people they employ.

Therefore, because all businesses have the same amount of time, we can only compare the remaining two resources, money and people. A simple ratio provides a wealth of information:

Productivity = Sales ÷ Number of Employees

Check it out compared to your competitors and your industry average. The key to your success is learning how you deploy and maximize the only two resources you have control over.

Think about this: In order to control and manage your time, you must first control and manage your resources. How do you do that?

Well, I would suggest time management. And if time management is the answer, project management is the tool.

The beauty of project management when properly configured for the job at hand is that it has an unparalleled track record of success in every field of public, private, and business endeavor since the 1950s.

Why? Because it works!

A project is simply a one-time event to accomplish a result. From business, manufacturing, and research and development to trade shows, the logic of defining what needs to be accomplished, who is responsible, and how it will be implemented has many benefits.

Your business is constantly identifying, innovating, modifying, and implementing your products and services. Controlling and managing how you develop and launch these new opportunities is based on time, money, and people.

Project management can get your products and services to market faster by identifying and creating the environment to streamline your processes, which reduces your risks, potential delays, and impediments to your success.

If you employ project management within your organization, you create your own unique strategic weapon. Your customers embrace your proactive strategy and flawless delivery, while your competitors wonder how you got to be so successful.

OBSERVATION

The planned three-week plant shutdown and relocation was about to commence in approximately one month. The company president called, and we discussed his relocation project. He asked if I had any suggestions.

I asked him if he considered this a project and if he would be interested in setting it up accordingly. He said, "We aren't building a space shuttle here, just relocating part of the business."

I pointed out that this relocation was no small task and required substantially more planning than just scheduling the machinery movers.

"What would you do differently?"

"I have a Five-Step Project Management System, and if you give me a couple of days, I will show you."

Two days later I was in his office presenting my project plan. In short, it was broken down into three phases:

1. New Facility Preparation

    1.1. Electrical, mechanical, and pneumatic considerations

1.2. Construction of the new offices and production areas

2. Plant Relocation Plan

    2.1. Project schedule with milestones

    2.2. Mapping machine tools with designated locations for machinery movers

    2.3. All electrical, mechanical, and pneumatic lines and connections installed prior to the actual move

3. Reinstallation and Start-up

    3.1. Final electrical, mechanical, and pneumatic connections

    3.2. Equipment start-up, test run, and debugging

    3.3. Sample qualification run(s) as needed

    3.4. QA/QC sign-off

The project started with initial equipment breakdown, while electricians disconnected equipment and the machinery movers transported equipment to the designated locations in the new facility. Each area and designated machine tool location was addressed in priority order and physically delivered back to front to maximize logics.

By pre-wiring the existing facility and running all mechanical lines prior to the actual move, we were able to simultaneously relocate the entire business and start up all machine tools by the following Sunday afternoon. Jobs interrupted were requalified by QA/QC during the relocation.

We were open for business. The team had moved the entire business across town and started the facility back up in three and a half days. The president remarked, "If I hadn't seen this myself, I would have never believed it. I don't know how you did this, but that project management stuff really works!"

OBSERVATION

Timely solutions are absolutely critical to your success. The CEO who plans the best, maximizes cost-effective resources, and concentrates on his or her business the most wins! It's that simple. But this plan of attack by itself is not action.

Although the results of inaction may not be immediately visible or measurable, in the end, they are always known and recordable. What's not all that simple, tough to recognize, and the recipe for disaster is thinking that *good* is good enough.

Don't limit yourself.

> Thinking good is *never* good enough!

INSIGHT 7

To be aware of the consequences of management indecision.

Are you in charge of your life and/or business?

One of my favorite questions to ask is "Who do you work for?"

Most people answer, "I work for the ABC or XYZ Company."

Interesting, but I ask again, "Who do your work for?"

Confused and perhaps somewhat irritated, they say it again: "I work for the ABC or XYZ Company."

"Really? Have you ever heard of ME, Incorporated?"

"No."

"That's precisely who you work for. Yourself!"

When you understand that the products and services you provide a company as the owner or employee is your business, it changes the way you conduct your business. You are in charge of management because you are the management of your company.

You are the chairman, chief executive officer (CEO), president, and largest shareholder of that personal business you call ME, Inc. It's your life and your choice how you deploy your resources, time, and money, and your investment with all the people you interact with on a daily, weekly, and monthly basis.

OBSERVATION

You are always going to make adjustments in your life or career, but are they relevant to the destination of your most certain direction? You can't plan for everything, and even if you could, the results may not manifest as planned. So why plan at all? Everything changes so fast that it may not be worth the effort to plan. That may be true, but planning gives you focus, and focus gives you the discipline to achieve your intended result at the end on the day.

You can never plan your way to a strategy, and therefore, you can only strategically take action or do nothing, regarding the actual results of your decision or indecision. All the data regarding the invasion on D-Day during the Second World War was cleverly disguised and totally misinterpreted by the enemy. For the United States and our Allies, it worked out well, and those monumental efforts saved the world, but for the bad guys it didn't turn out as they intended.

The point is never relying on data alone.

Inadequate attention to detail and inadequate safeguards create hesitation and the resulting potential management indecision(s). At the end of the day, any problems, questions, issues, or concerns are always the result of management's actions and/or inactions.

Why is it different in business but not in your personal life? Here are three questions that will continually challenge you and your career:

1. What do you really want in your career and in life and why?

2. How are you going to achieve those goals and objectives?

3. When do you expect to achieve a successful result?

INSIGHT 8

To realize in business that everything is a performance issue.

CEOs need to focus on what can make their organizations successful. Your sole responsibility is to lead the organization, acquire new customers, and capitalize on new opportunities to generate the revenue, growth, and profitability you correctly anticipated. You need to continually make things happen!

During the start-up phase, you probably had the privilege of performing all the tasks from sales, marketing, engineering, quality assurance and control, accounting, and human resources to lawn care, the always exciting trash removal, and the ever-popular bathroom patrol.

But as the business continued to grow, you began to be painfully aware of the storm clouds fast approaching that could potentially impede your success. You experienced growing pains (change) that constricted your ability to respond effectively to your customers' expectations.

It was then you realized that you had to make a decision. If you believed your customer depended on your performance, you had to ask yourself a question: "Are you going to continue in the role of the technical expert or actually run the company?"

Few can perform both, and most eventually make the correct decision only too late.

If you own and/or run a business, you already know what 24/7 means. It doesn't mean twenty-four hours a day, seven days a week. It means total dedication, and total dedication means having the discipline to get the job done. It also means having the courage of your convictions in spite of that early start-up and cash-flow nightmares questioning your desire to continue. Along the way, you learned total dedication to continual improvement.

Only people who have survived long enough to successfully cash flow their operation actually make it. Unfortunately, many make that one fatal mistake and lose it all. Worst-case scenario: their business, home, and family.

Consider these phrases: "Your Olympics begin today," "Failure is not an option," "Second place means first loser," and "You will not fail." All are tidbits of wisdom you may have heard before, but are they relevant to your situation? Do they mean anything to you? The one thing these tidbits of wisdom all have in common is total dedication.

That spirit always carries over and is reflected in your character, attitude, and work ethic. Your employees and customers have a front-row seat on the observation deck and don't miss much. They see reality. Do you plan accordingly?

Remember, if it's not important to you, how can you expect it to be important to your employees? Your coworkers? Your customers? Your friends? Your family?

The reality is you may in fact be the technical expert in your organization, but you may not actually be the best leader for the organization's needs in the future.

If you think you are in the elite group of leaders who actually perform both the technical and managerial functions at the highest levels … fantastic! Please continue.

OBSERVATION

During a sales presentation to a potential client, the client commented that she liked what was being discussed but questioned my understanding of her business. I simply said, "I know what it's like to stare at the ceiling at two forty-five in the morning trying to figure out how I was going to make payroll."

The client quite literally flew out her chair, leaned across her desk, and said, "You know exactly what I am talking about! You really do understand my business."

The only difference between companies, no matter what their size, is the amount of revenue earned (Sales) and the number of people they employ. Remember, as they say, "Business is business," and all businesses have the same three resources: time, money, and people. Use them wisely!

Here's the bottom line:

1. If you think you should be doing better, why aren't you?

2. And if you know you aren't doing better than you should be, why haven't you changed?

3. It's only when you change that things will change for you!

> It's your time and money, so it's ultimately your choice!

INSIGHT 9

To understand and practice the Five Laws of Business religiously.

One day I took out a file and started thumbing through my notes, looking for some ideas for an article. I have been to many strategic-planning classes, workshops, and meetings, but none gave me a simple method to remember, communicate, and implement the strategies effectively back at the office. So I developed what I called the Five Laws of Business.

FIRST LAW OF BUSINESS: VISION

The recognition and confirmation of the customer's need(s):

> … for the Customer

A general recognition or anticipation of a need(s) and a general plan to meet that need(s) in order to gain customer commitment.

> … for the Business

Periodically reviewing that need(s) to confirm its validity and the plans to support the overall vision of the business.

>... for the Strategy

Short, clearly expressed statement of the purpose, goal(s), and objective(s) of the organization and its plan(s) for achievement.

SECOND LAW OF BUSINESS: MISSION

>The Strategic Plan

Defines the mission—the who, what, where, when, why, and how this will work.

THIRD LAW OF BUSINESS: COMMON SENSE

>Revenue – Expense = What? (Pop quiz)

FOURTH LAW OF BUSINESS: LEADERSHIP

The discipline to balance revenue, growth, and profitability throughout the organization.

Operations (sales, engineering, customer service, manufacturing, maintenance, etc.).

- + Accounting/Financial Management
- + Sales and Marketing
- + Technology (MIS/IT, CAD/CAM, LASER, FMS, etc.)
- + Quality Assurance/Quality Control
- + <u>Staffing, Benefits, Insurance, and Policies (Human Resources)</u>
- = Revenue, Growth, and Profitability

FIFTH LAW OF BUSINESS: PERSEVERANCE

Mastering perseverance and the attributes of the Five Laws of Business ensures success!

- ♪ Always be enthusiastic.
- ♪ Never stop selling your product, service, or yourself.
- ♪ Always treat people with respect.
- ♪ Never stop learning and improving.
- ♪ Always honor your commitments.
- ♪ Always collect what's due on a timely basis.

Always pay your bills on time.

OBSERVATION

Why is perseverance in paying your bills on time so important? Because if you strive to pay your bills on time and have the capacity to do so, it clearly demonstrates that your operation is in control and your operations, accounting/financial management, sales and marketing, technology, QA/QC, and human resources are all contributing to your organization's revenue, growth, and profitability.

Think of it this way: In order for you to be able to pay your bills on time, you must be executing the Five Laws of Business efficiently and effectively. If you cannot pay your bills on time, you may run the risk of not being able to pay them at all.

Pay attention to your receivables; they're the foundation of your cash flow.

> Bad news scenarios can't happen if you actually practice the Five Laws of Business.

PART 3

Leadership Principles

INSIGHT 1

To recognize that luck is preparation meeting opportunity and is always an unstoppable force when driven by the proper attitude.

Performance reviews are typically subjective, numerical venues that always left me wondering how this could actually improve an individual's performance. These subjective and/or numerical reviews are typically based on the individual's performance during the past two weeks. Numerical reviews leave you in the gap between three and four or four and five (with five being the highest).

The ultimate insults in my opinion were MBOs (Management by Objectives), which were disasters on their way to happening. The goals and objectives supposedly agreed to with management were not necessarily in my control or the control of the manager, supervisor, or employee.

Managers or supervisors typically rely on standardized definitions to assess performance, which may have little to do with an individual's actual performance. In fact, standardized definitions may be contrary to the best interests of the individual and company. For example, many long-standing employees have been relieved of their duties simply because they did not achieve standardized definitions.

I have no problem with eliminating personnel who have stopped learning or excelling in their positions, but I have a big problem with eliminating personnel under the pretense of reducing costs.

The 360 peer reviews have the best intentions, but all too often they are a popularity contest or a means to eliminate the one person who is actually trying to change the status quo and make things happen.

I have always believed the job/performance review should actually reflect an individual's performance based on his or her goals and/or objectives in relation to the company's goals and/or objectives, not the manager or supervisor's goals and/or objectives alone. Certainly, course corrections may be warranted and/or advisable, but not at years end! Discussing performance issues a year or two later is a totally meaningless exercise and a waste of time.

Your employees' performance, depending on their position and/or interactions with the customer may look great and sound great to you, but your customers may have a totally different opinion of your employees' performance when it comes to their cost, quality, and delivery. By not addressing the root cause of less-than-expected performance, you have failed at one of the most crucial parts of your position.

As leaders, it's your responsibility to accomplish assigned tasks on time and within budget. However, in order to hit those budgets in the majority of cases, we must work with and through people. If your employees are only performing tasks to complete your mission without knowing the game plan, how can you expect your charges to measure their expected performance in a meaningful manner when they have had no input to begin with? How is that helping the individual or ultimately the customer?

Here is an opportunity for consideration: Instead of just assigning new and/or unfamiliar tasks, ask the individual if he or she is interested in learning or solving a problem. For example, why weren't perceived or identified problems, issues, questions, and/or concerns addressed previously? If these considerations were addressed, why haven't the solutions been developed and implemented? Or if the solutions have been developed and implemented, why haven't they worked? If they have worked, what can we learn from this exercise?

One of your most important roles is that of being a mentor to the next generation of leadership. This is a win-win proposition for the individual, the team, the company, and the customer. An individual may have years of experience, specific knowledge, and skills that are utilized during daily activities, which are truly beneficial to your organization, but only lacks the specific education and training to excel in his or her current or new assignments.

This is a no-brainer. You give me a person who is committed to continual learning and achieving, and is willing to work, and I have just put money in the bank and developed a role model for the rest of the enterprise. Sounds like a good investment to me. Don't you agree?

OBSERVATION

During a management team meeting, I asked this question: "Can you give me a one-word definition of success?"

We went around the conference table with answers ranging from good health, winning the lottery, and job promotion to purchasing a new car, winning a new car or house, and completing a college degree. Approximately twenty answers came to mind from the seven members of the management team. I recorded these on a flip chart.

Then I said, "I have a second question for you, a little bit different from the first. Give me a one-word definition of success, but you can't use any of the words written on this flip chart." Now it got a little tougher. We went around the conference table again, and the group did manage to come up with another four or five ideas.

This time I said, "One last question. Give me a one-word definition of success, but you can't use any of these words written on this flip chart."

I then asked each person if he or she had any other ideas. Dead silence. No additional suggestions seemed to be forthcoming, so I said, "Would a reasonable person agree that in general the words on the flip chart give a reasonable definition of success, realizing we could take all afternoon parsing words?" Everyone smiled and nodded in agreement.

"So do you feel comfortable with these definitions?"

Again everyone smiled and nodded in agreement.

"Would anyone like to add or delete from the list?"

No one did.

I said, "Let me tell you something about comfort. When you are comfortable, aren't you coasting? And when you are coasting, aren't you going downhill?"

Therefore, never get comfortable. Remember the shark?

> Continual learning never stops
> and neither should you!

INSIGHT 2

To never allow yourself to get married to a business idea.

One of the reasons you have a board of directors is to secure divergent thought. Many times the butcher, baker, candlestick maker, attorney, insurance broker, CPA, engineer, and/or banker are invited to a board meeting for their business acumen, technical, and/or legal/financial expertise.

That's all well and good, but you also have a workforce consisting of sometimes decades of real-world experience. The board of directors is not the only resource available to the company. Invite your company's personnel in first and consider their insights appropriately.

A changing world drives continual improvement. The days of the command-and-control business models have long passed. Today, business needs all the help it can get. Certainly money is important, but reward and recognition also work wonders when implemented correctly and may pay dividends far beyond the gift card.

Being receptive to your employees' ideas and/or opinions is not only good business but it's also free!

OBSERVATION

Don't become a one-trick pony.

Engineering gets old if all you're doing is updating and/or modifying old designs and products. That may have worked years ago but not today and definitely not for long. It's probably not a good business model unless you are in the repair business.

Here's another example: Conventional wisdom and protocols dictated that scrap in manufacturing would be identified with a red tag. As we toured the plant, the gentleman from the government agency said, "I don't see any red tags. How do you identify your nonconforming parts or scrap?"

"Sir, we don't make scrap. We may err on occasion and create nonconforming product, but we don't make scrap."

He pondered that for a second and asked, "So how do you identify your nonconforming product?"

"Nonconforming product is marked with black tags and placed in a holding area until QA/QC makes the final disposition regarding its status."

He said, "Great, why black?"

"Black is less visible. We all know it's there, but we also know this is a manufacturing facility and mistakes will occur, but why focus on it? Red means danger and a constant reminder of our failure to meet the customer's expectations. I would much rather have employees focus on not creating nonconforming product in the first place, rather than constantly being reminded of our failures. In fact, we tag each job with green tags just to emphasize the quality and professionalism of our workforce."

I found the negative reminder (red tags) created a negative atmosphere. It's not that everyone ignored the nonconforming issues; we just fixed the problem and moved on. I know it's a mind game, but why in the world would you broadcast your errors/failures to your employees and customers?

You always perform to the expectations you set for yourself. Our team knew its goal was simply to reduce and/or eliminate black-tagged parts/product from occurring. At the end of the day, the team did.

Simple enough when you think about it:

> Does it really matter what color the tag is?

INSIGHT 3

To remember that listening is the other half of communication.

During a brainstorming meeting, the corporate trainer asked for ideas from those assembled. The ideas ranged from reduced setups to complete review of the products to streamlining the manufacturing processes.

By the time it was my turn to add to the general discussion, I felt the corporate trainer may have been hoping for answers from a different perspective and direction than the group was going. They were all good ideas, but they were the standard engineering/manufacturing answers. In my opinion, they all lacked vision, which was why I thought the trainer was facilitating this meeting in the first place.

I was next, so without hesitation I said, "We must never stop asking why—why are we not looking for new technology and processes to improve our products and services; why are we meeting again and again to rehash the same ideas; why are the quality systems we have in place today not doing anything to solve any of the real problems?"

The corporate trainer said, "Interesting, but I was looking for specifics not generalizations."

I said, "You can't get specifics to solve the problem if you are only solving the symptoms. In other words, if you don't or can't identify the real problem, you will be dancing around the solutions dartboard for a long time."

Today, those fundamental questions are known as the Five-Why Root Cause Analysis or a thousand other diagnostic descriptions all of which are implemented by companies actively seeking continual improvement.

OBSERVATION

If you can't be an adult and professional, how can you expect to win the respect of your peers? When symbolism over substance is the name of the game, everyone rallies around the "at least we are trying to do something" school of business. Ever wonder why it's hard to motivate your employees when they know nothing is going to change? They have seen this insightful management rollout before. From their viewpoint, past experience dictates this attitude of no commitment, which for whatever reason seems to be the safest bet.

What a poor way to think about winning and success in the workplace. Work without meaning is far more than frustrating; it's the kiss of death for you and your company. Star performers eventually will leave because they can't get anything done.

You need to seek out and work with the winners, who make contributions to the company's success. Otherwise you are just wasting your time, and it's costing you a lot more money than you may think. Seek out those who are not only recognized for their accomplishments, but genuinely take pride in their results and are not afraid to pass along that knowledge, skill, expertise, and experience to others.

> If you apply yourself and continually increase the value of your knowledge, skill, expertise, and experience, you will never have to worry about a paycheck.

INSIGHT 4

To practice the art of MBWA (management by walking around), rather than the science of illusion.

As we walked along during a plant tour, I noticed a lot of self-promotional banners and posters all over the facility. You have seen them—"The Customer is #1" or "Our Goal Is Total Customer Satisfaction." Some had a bit of humor, and one banner even had the company's mission statement. Well, you get the picture.

I asked the company president if he would mind sharing how he developed his mission statement. He said, "You can ask anyone in this company about our mission statement." As we continued, he elaborated that the company had spent fourteen months and a considerable amount of money getting all employees involved in developing the mission statement.

So when I was introduced to one of the employees, I said, "I noticed your banners and posters and wanted to know about your mission statement."

The first thing she said was "We spent fourteen months and a considerable amount of money defining our mission. The entire company was involved. It was a real team effort. We all carry these vest pocket cards with our mission statement. Everyone in the company has a card."

She was beaming with pride. The president was beaming with pride. Everybody was beaming.

The vest pocket cards were put together beautifully, but unfortunately what they had, in my opinion, was not a mission statement. What they had really created, or what it had morphed into, was the corporate mantra and the basis for internal cheerleading. That's not a mission statement.

Most mission statements are *vision* statements, i.e., the thirty-thousand-foot view of their impression of themselves and/or how they intended to fulfill the needs and expectations of the customer. I asked how their mission statement helped the customer, because I could not find or could I see any evidence of specifically addressing the needs and expectations of the customer in any of their banners and posters, or the mission statement itself.

If it doesn't answer the questions of who, what, where, when, why, and how the mission is to be accomplished, it is not a mission statement; it's a vision statement.

The president asked if I wanted to continue the tour. Actually I thought we might be done. We were. We marched right back to the front office where we exchanged pleasantries and I left. He obviously did not like the fact that I brought this reality check to his attention.

About a year later he called and asked to meet. It was a much different and very productive meeting that time.

OBSERVATION

Simply put, MBWA means continually searching for new ideas and resolutions to actual and perceived problems. It does not mean being a social butterfly to make people feel good for a minute or two.

If you are not asking questions of your shop floor personnel, you are missing a wonderful opportunity to see and hear what's really happening on a daily basis. Many times managers and supervisors give directives and/or instructions but rarely ask questions. When you don't ask questions, aren't you in essence avoiding reality because you are not interested, engaged, or care enough to even listen?

Don't settle or compromise your values and principles for short-term, low rewards and inconsequential gains because you can get away with it. In order to reap the benefits of all the resources available, you must capitalize on the opportunities to leapfrog the competition. How do you do that? You should never stop selling yourself or your product or service, and most importantly never sell yourself short.

Remember, you can gain a great deal of knowledge by simply understanding that ...

Listening is the other half of communication.

INSIGHT 5

To know tomorrow is important, but today is critical to your success.

If I had a dollar for every time I heard "I don't have time for this" or "Where am I supposed to find the time to get that done?" we would all be enjoying the sunset, listening to the waves, and sipping tall cool ones. How many variations of those phrases have you heard? Not enough times to warrant your consideration?

Oh please!

I always wondered how in the world people found the time to fix the problem, but they never had enough time to prevent the problem in the first place. This modus operandi is called firefighting, and it has nothing to do with your local fire department.

The fundamental problem here is time management and poor planning. Time is the only resource you can never make up. Once it's gone, it's gone! Yes, you can work overtime or add extra personnel to catch up, but at what cost?

Is scrambling your game plan of choice?

That's your strategy?

Sometimes it is necessary but not as a standard operating procedure (SOP).

The big question at the end of the day is "Was it worth it?" The extra cost, the aggravation, and the projection of poor leadership. In some very specific cases or circumstances, it may be absolutely necessary and critical to work overtime, while at other times not as critical and/or necessary as it first appeared to be.

Let's look at this from a different direction. What's a minute worth? Not much by itself, but that also depends on the context. For example, it may be the difference between life and death, success and failure, or winning and losing.

In your business, if your shop rate is sixty dollars an hour, a minute is worth one dollar. So what does that mean? What's the point?

BASIS OF PRODUCTIVITY

Shop Rate = $60/Hour
$60/Hour ÷ 60 Minutes = $1.00/Minute
Example 50 Employees

    50   X   8 Hrs/Day   =   400 Total Hours/Day (Potential Productivity)
    400   X   60 Minutes/Hour   =   24,000 Minutes/Day (Potential Productivity)
    24,000   X   95% Efficient X 95% Effective = 21,660 Minutes/Day (Actual Productivity)
24,000 - 21,660 = 2,340 Minutes/Day X $1/Minute = $2,340/Day (Lost $$$ of Productivity/Day)
$2,340 X 250 Workdays = $585,000/60 Minutes/Hour = 9,750 Hours (Lost Hours of Productivity/Year)

But look what happens when you only increase your efficiency and effectiveness by 1 percent, using the same example:

Shop Rate = $60/Hour
$60/Hour ÷ 60 Minutes = $1.00/Minute
Example 50 Employees

    50   X   8 Hrs/Day   =   400 Total Hours/Day (Potential Productivity)
   400   X   60 Minutes/Hour   =   24,000 Minutes/Day (Potential Productivity)
24,000   X   96% Efficient X 96% Effective = 22,118 Minutes/Day (Actual Productivity)
24,000 - 22,118 = 1,882 Minutes/Day X $1/Minute = $1,882/Day (Lost $$$ of Productivity/Day)
$1,882 X 250 Workdays = $470,500/60 Minutes/Hour = 7,842 Hours (Lost Hours of Productivity/Year)

POTENTIAL SAVINGS (PRODUCTIVITY THAT YIELDS "MAGIC")

9,750 Hours - 7,842 Hours = **1,908 Hours (Potentially Saved)**

$585,000 - $470,500 = **$114,500 (Potentially Saved)**

With only a 1 percent increase in your efficiency and effectiveness, you will yield a substantial benefit. Wouldn't you love to have those 1,908 hours at the end of your year to bill?

Look at this:

Shop Rate $/Hr.	Hours	Potential Billings
25	1,908	**$47,700**
50	1,908	**$95,400**
75	1,908	**$143,100**
100	1,908	**$190,800**
125	1,908	**$238,500**

Now what's a minute worth?

OBSERVATION

Cost reductions are static, i.e., once accounted for their relevance, further cost reductions may be limited or nonexistent.

It doesn't matter what product or service your business sells or provides, and it doesn't matter how many dollars you make. It's what you keep that counts!

Look at the example above and try to justify why it will not pay dividends. Nobody is making so much money that they can't afford to look at each minute as a contributing factor in the profit of their operation. Conversely, nobody is making so much money that they can afford constant errors or rework. It costs approximately three to four times the original cost to correct the error or rework, thus reducing your profit. If you are smart enough to earn that kind of money, you are smart enough to prevent the potential loss in the first place.

Once you understand what a minute is worth, it's amazing how that brings things into focus just like compound interest. Both have a magic of their own.

What steps have you taken to reduce inefficiencies and ineffectiveness? Do your employees have the proper tools and equipment to perform at their best? As the leader of the company, division, or team, have you engaged your employees to make contributions to their own job security and that of the company?

Don't just strive do it right the first time, do it right all the time.

We all know time is money, so make the decision today and don't wait for tomorrow to implement it!

INSIGHT 6

To set your goals and objectives just out of reach, but not out of sight.

A written business plan is simply your goals and objectives stated with action plans, measurements, milestones, and implementation processes to achieve those stated goals and objectives.

I asked the owner of a company if he had a business plan. "All companies have a business plan," he said. Of course all companies have a business plan; they are just not all written down. Those that are written down may be on a shelf, in a drawer, or simply kept a secret.

Actually, the owner was just finishing up his business plan, and when it was completed, he would "Give it to his management team."

Really?

How much buy-in do you think he will get from his management team? If you surmised little to none, you are today's winner!

In order to develop a workable, relevant, and agreed-to business plan, you need to understand how to set goals and objectives for the greatest potential of achievement. Goals and objectives can be thought of as a "purpose statement." Purpose is the hi-tech fuel that provides the energy and momentum in our lives. Without purpose, we would have a tough time getting any intended result.

Sounds simple enough, doesn't it?

Just set goals and objectives and achieve them. However, without purpose you can't get great results, and it's those great results that inform the world and enhance your reputation. For the salaried among us, that's what we get paid for—*results*!

Management by objectives (MBO) was the classic game plan of the month and the fad of the year some time ago. How could any responsible person who expects his or her personnel to totally commit to someone else's goals and objectives—or know how to attain them—without understanding why they were important is destined for failure. That methodology may work in the military and alphabet soup agencies, but not so well in the business world.

The individual was being held accountable for *x*, *y*, and *z*, but had virtually little or no control and certainly not the authority to accomplish that goal or objective. In some instances, the employee had to sign his or her MBOs, which then made it a contract, in my opinion. Bad news for the "at will" mind-set as outlined in your typical employee's handbook. Let's just say it caused a lot of problems and finally disappeared into management's circular file of 'Underappreciated Visionary Excellence'. The company's highly touted strategy really upset hardworking dedicated employees and eventually led to total failure.

OBSERVATION

As the leader, shouldn't your goal be to help those in your charge? Remember, it's their *actual* performance that counts, not your version of what you remember. What were the results of their assessment? The one-through-five or five-through-ten numerical assessment scale is always based on the past two to four weeks. If nothing of consequence happened and you have no goals or objectives, it's tough to measure any performance issues. So if it's not written down, what is the basis of your performance review?

No major hiccups?

No people problems?

So everyone is beaming?

Good job!

A performance review is fundamentally a communication tool. When used properly, performance can be evaluated and milestones can be established and discussed openly and honestly, with both parties making significant contributions to their professional development and continual improvement of the company.

Achieving goals and/or objectives is a cathartic experience if done for the right reason (purpose). Winning without trying is the guaranteed path to emptiness. For example, you may have the knowledge, skills, expertise, and experience to perform the task, but without the courage to start and discipline to continue, you will never achieve your intended result.

If you are not totally committed to your goal and objective you will fall short. If you are doing it for someone else, you had better have a clear picture of how and why your efforts will be recognized and what the benefit will be—not necessarily today but certainly in the near future. If you are not thinking like this, you are wasting your time.

And the old adage, "Time Is Money," really means just that. You can never make up the time, and therefore, you may never make up the money.

> Rather than trying to accomplish *everything* without building a foundation for success, achieving small, directed incremental goals and objectives successfully has a far greater probability of providing the basis for hitting your target.

INSIGHT 7

To work on the correct things rather than the important things.

Everything is important, but not everything is equally important. Determining the "correct things" can be totally challenging at best or totally frustrating in the worst-case scenario. The trick is to determine what is critical to your success and work solely on that aspect of your game plan.

How do you make a decision? It all starts with identifying the problem, issue, question, concern, or your goal and/or objective in the decision-making process.

Are you just going along to get along? Not exactly the definition of leadership. Do you gather enough information to make a creditable decision? Do you educate yourself and potentially become the company's subject matter expert? Or do you procrastinate making the decision because of the fear of failure or the unknown consequences of being unpopular?

Again, not exactly the qualities of leadership you would want to emulate.

OBSERVATION

Looking around the conference table, I couldn't place the distracting sound. No one seemed concerned, but it was certainly odd. Then it happened again, only louder. Now I really started looking around when suddenly the gentleman across the conference table said, "I no longer work for the company," and pointed to the wall clock.

I'm thinking to myself, you have got to be kidding!

I quickly learned we had project members who were communicating that it was the end of their day and they were ready to go home. As far as they were concerned, the meeting was over. Not only that but they got up, excused themselves, and said we could continue the meeting in the morning.

Say what?

After entering the CEO's office and exchanging pleasantries, I explained the situation and the criticality of the time factor, as I was only there for one week. He understood, and the next day we finished up the day's meetings when the topics and action plan were completed, all parties present.

Believe me, no one was beaming.

In the long run, it worked out. The start-up of the new facility was accomplished within one week of the projected fifteen-month date in spite of all the roadblocks and potholes, but getting to that point really ruffled a lot of feathers.

> If you can actually manage your time correctly, you can consider yourself successful because you are managing the correct things.

INSIGHT 8

To be aware of new technology and how it will affect your future.

You would be amazed how many companies have computers but little to no automation of their business systems, with the exception of payroll, general ledger, purchasing, inventory, and sales order entry.

You know, "Spreadsheets rule!"

You would be even more amazed at how many companies have ERP (Enterprise Resource Planning) software but have never implemented all the modules. You may also be amazed at how many companies think training is education and education is expensive and therefore not necessary.

Training is the mechanics, and education provides the platform to understand those mechanics when applying the principles to resolve a problem or execute the task at hand.

You probably have heard the term "learn by doing" as a training method, but the problem is not everyone learns at the same rate or in the same manner. Some learn by observation, some by listening, some by study, and some by hearing. If that is true, then education and training (E&T) may take longer to achieve results than originally anticipated, which of course complicate the learning curve.

Without laying the proper foundation, introducing new technology is introducing change, and change without preparation can be a real-life fatal business nightmare. All the latest technology in the world will never alleviate the fear of change via implementation not addressed.

OBSERVATION

An accounting firm asked if I could investigate why its client had decided to return the ERP software that had been installed the previous month. The individual modules had been installed correctly and worked well, but the overall system did not perform as advertised. The software was a known commodity and had a great reputation. So why wasn't it working for this company?

"Good question," I said. "Let's find out."

Speaking to each of the users, their individual module was in fact working, but they were all having difficulties with speed, access, and getting meaningful reports. By the time I got to the accounting department, I was really confused until I discovered the accounting module was installed but never used.

The problem wasn't the software or the users but the non-utilization of one module to fully integrate the system. Instead of simply refunding the money for the software, I asked if appropriate company personnel would like to "go back to school" at no additional expense to the client. The accounting firm agreed to a one-week training program at its facility and then a one-week, on-site follow-up training program to set up the company's accounts, payroll, and so on.

The accounting firm was happy, the company was happy, and the president was relieved.

> Your agility in fulfilling the customers' needs and expectations is your job security!

INSIGHT 9

To demand simple strategies to resolve problems, questions, issues, and concerns.

Keep in mind, there are thousands of so-called experts in business. People think they have become experts because they teach it or have made some money. But in my lifetime, I have only known one person who meets both the technical and managerial functions at the highest levels. He was an innovator, an international business leader with the knowledge and skills to continue the tradition of excellence established by his family's business over a hundred years ago. And boy was he successful.

Charles W. Finkl, chairman and CEO of A. Finkl & Sons, a pioneer in the steel and forging industry, was the epitome of the word *professional*.

During my three and a half years of working with Chuck, I really learned what thinking beyond the obvious meant. Chuck once told me, "It was pretty easy to become the president of the company when your dad owned it." True, but his father, William Finkl, didn't subscribe to the Peter Principle philosophy of management. William Finkl understood what the expression "revenue minus expenses" meant, and he made *damn* sure Chuck understood and lived that philosophy too. Consequently, Chuck worked his way up through the company for twenty-five years before becoming the president of A. Finkl & Sons.

While I was working in plant engineering at the company, no matter how well thought-out my designs, proposals, or game plans were, Chuck always had a question that sent me back to the drawing board. I was young with an attitude of invincibility, so I had a tough time getting over the fact that my ideas were rejected so quickly. I thought there might be some kind of a message or lesson there, but what it was I hadn't a clue. What I did know was that rejection was a word that almost made me stop trying and put an end to my career.

Hey, I was twenty-six years old. I had done a lot of things by that time and thought I knew a lot of stuff. Did I know everything? Well, let's just say I thought I did! Actually I didn't as was proven on numerous occasions.

However, I also knew my ideas couldn't be totally wrong or that far off. So I decided that I would change my approach and never stop pitching my ideas, no matter how many times they got shot down. I was going to use rejection as a reality check rather than the indicator of my ingenious failures. You can't hit the game-winning home run if you don't step up to the plate and start swinging.

For example, a forging was difficult to secure during the sawing operation. Looking at the prints and watching how shop personnel actually cut the forging, I had an idea. Three simple tooling fixtures would accommodate the various sizes within a group or family, and interchangeability would reduce setup time considerably. The design engineer thought it was a great idea and said, "Put it on paper."

I drew up detailed prints, and the plant engineer reviewed the idea. "Looks good to me," he said. "Let's see what Chuck thinks."

In my cartoon bubble, I thought, "Oh boy, here we go again!"

Standing in the president's office, once more I felt this overwhelming sense of regret that I had pushed this concept so hard. Did I forget something? My mind was racing. Would this be another one of those situations where I didn't have the answer to a question I had not thought of or prepared for yet? Chuck was busy but took the time to invite us in to look at this proposal. He studied the prints intently for several minutes.

"Cost?" he asked.

I explained that by building all three tooling fixtures, we would cover the entire range of products with a 20 percent buffer for future sizes within each family. The cost would be less than $19,000 for all three fixtures. We would save approximately fourteen minutes per setup and achieve payback within four and half months based on current sales. The investment would generate a 37 percent ROI (Return on Investment).

Silence. Absolute, drop-dead silence.

In those microseconds, rejection was raising its ugly head again. I thought he was going to say, "Forget it!"

For a second, however, I wasn't sure if I had actually heard what I thought I just heard. Confidence wasn't yet the driver in my life, and of course my good friend Mr. Self-Doubt was ever-present whispering in my ear.

Chuck said, "We have been struggling with this for years. Go ahead; build it! Good job!"

Eventually I became an expert at having viable alternatives with supporting facts. Occasionally I got sent back to the drawing board, but the questions became fewer and fewer. I was no longer looking to solve *a* symptom; I was looking to solve *the* problem. With Chuck's help, I had discovered the magic of "looking beyond the obvious."

OBSERVATION

Many have made the comment that I see things differently. And I do. A colleague once commented that I got to the bottom line faster than anyone he had ever known. In other words, I am a realist. I see things the way they are, not as I may think they are, hope they are, or want them to be.

When addressing a problem, issue, question, or concern, I make sure all of my questions are definitely thought-provoking. To arrive at the solution, the questions may be simple, but the answers are generally complex and require a great deal of thought. Some may consider this confrontational. I consider it challenging the status quo and the basis for continual improvement. Hopefully this sparks thought, investigation, and action.

To this day, I am in the ever-present teaching mode. My intent is to pass along this gift to all those who are willing to listen and learn. I didn't realize it at the time, but Chuck was actually teaching me to look beyond the obvious in all things at all times. That included how to handle rejection.

Simple is always the best approach to solving a problem. Why make the solution so complicated that it slows or stops progress toward the actual problem's resolution? If you look beyond the obvious, you may find that you have actually identified the real problem, issue, question, or concern and therefore have a higher probability of solving it.

I realized long ago that I was not Chuck Finkl by any stretch of the imagination, but I have always tried to live up to the standards he established. I have always tried to lead from the front, expect the best, and set the example I would follow. I was proud to be considered his friend. He will be missed.

So here's my simple recipe for success:

> Failure presents new opportunities, and rejection is only an opportunity disguised as a problem.

INSIGHT 10

To lead, encourage, and motivate with rewards and recognition.

I asked my secretary to see me when she had a minute. When she entered my office, I asked her to take a seat. I had an idea I wanted to run by her and ask for her opinion.

Sales and Marketing had a position opening, and I wanted to know if she had given any thought to applying. She acknowledged the position's opening but had decided not to apply.

"May I ask why?" I said.

"Well, I have never worked in Sales and Marketing and don't know anything about computers."

I said, "So what's the problem?"

"Well, I really can't apply for a job I'm not qualified for, can I?"

That may be technically accurate for certain positions, such as a doctor, lawyer, engineer, or CPA, but I said, "I think you are qualified and you should apply. What's the worst thing that can happen? You don't get the position?"

"What if we looked at this differently? What would you learn from this experience if you didn't get the position?"

She said, "Well, I would know what I needed to qualify for the position."

"True, but what else? You have been with the company for over fifteen years. You are the company's expert in the customers' requirements and documentation. You know the customers, their products, and the contacts. I believe you are qualified. You are just not up to speed with the new technology (computers) yet. For example, you are great at organization and planning.

"Do you think Sales and Marketing could utilize your organizational and planning skills? Do you think Sales and Marketing could utilize your investigative and research skills? You have the knowledge, skills, and track record to perform the essential functions of this position. The only thing you need to do is apply them and learn Sales and Marketing speak. I think you would be the perfect candidate!"

She chuckled apprehensively. "What about the computer?"

"Just enroll in some computer classes. Find the course and get signed up."

She said, "Okay, I'll give it a try!"

OBSERVATION

She made the decision to look beyond the obvious. A few night classes later, our new Sales and Marketing assistant was running the show. She also went on to perform other jobs and positions for which she wasn't qualified either!

In order to lead, encourage, and motivate, you need to create new opportunities for your employees that challenge their potential while complementing your revenue, growth, and profitability game plans. The only limits encumbering your goals, objectives, and lifestyle are the ones you place on yourself and accept. Knowing what you need is not as important as knowing you can get it and then going for it!

If you change,
things will change for you!

INSIGHT 11

To resolve internal conflicts respectfully and immediately!

Without delving into the clinical definition of *conflict* resolution, you could think of it in terms of these analogies: a priest, rabbi, or minister trying to save a marriage; the third person in bar fight; a hostage negotiator trying to resolve a situation; or the first police officer through the door in a domestic dispute. I think you get the picture. The scenarios are endless—some stressful, some extremely dangerous.

Oh! Wait a minute. What about workplace violence?

You all have heard stories of individuals who have been downsized from large corporations. Now they're working for you, but they are still mentally engaged at the old job. Fortunately for you, they always let you know they are worth far more than what they're currently being paid and believe they are definitely worth it.

There is a problem with this type of self-promotion. At the end of the day, it's self-destructive and potentially creates a dangerous situation in the workplace if taken to the extreme. And that is the scary part. All this may be smoldering below the surface. Caution: Where there is smoke, there is fire. And like the fire beneath the surface, you can't see electricity. And like electricity, people can blow a fuse!

When I had heard about one employee's recent temper tantrums and poor behavior, I asked the individual to come to my office. My intention was to uncover the real problem and defuse the situation. There is an old saying that goes "Expect the unexpected."

I grew up in Chicago, and my radar was working overtime just before he came across my desk. My defense mechanisms immediately kicked in, and I halted his forward progress. I told him in a cool, calm, collected, and rather loud command-and-control voice to *sit down* or I was going to help him out the front door that instant!

In retrospect that's what I should have done immediately. However, at the time, I just wanted to calm him down. We talked. I answered all his questions politely, honestly, and professionally, but I again made it clear that the dollars and benefits were not changing. I told him we needed his knowledge, skills, and expertise, but our budget would never match his previous employer's in the short term. I reminded him that we covered all of these problems, questions, issues, and/or concerns during the interview process. I know he considered these carefully because he told me so when he accepted the position.

At the end of the day, he needed the job, but it was not working out as he had envisioned. He was frustrated to be sure, but he also needed to know that kind of behavior was not going to be tolerated no matter where he worked.

He immediately made the decision to leave the company and thanked me for taking the time to at least hear him out. He apologized and left.

OBSERVATION

This is not the kind of problem that is necessarily on the surface, but left unaddressed it can be in short order. People can put up with many things at work, except knowing they are not being treated as professionals or respected.

To this day, I firmly believe being respectful and resolving the problem, issue, question or concern immediately works best. I made it a policy to have a simple, informal meeting at the end of a new hire's first two weeks and the end of his or her first month. This gave both parties (the new hire and the hiring manager and/or supervisor) a chance to assess the individual's performance to date in relation to their mutual expectations, thus preventing future problems.

Generally, most people have pride in themselves, their craft, and their job. Most people are proud of the work they perform. Shouldn't you be proud of them?

> In order to attain that high level of performance throughout your organization, you need to always look beyond the obvious.

INSIGHT 12

To always lead from the front and expect the best!

Like you, I have made my fair share of mistakes, but I always learned to get up, brush myself off, and forge ahead. The view looking up was never as great as the view from the top. Do that enough times and you tend become knowledgeable, skilled, and experienced fast. People notice that you anticipate, bring things to the discussion for substantive consideration, and have a different way of looking at things. Coworkers may think you are really smart, and you may be, but just remember that your manager and/or supervisor in all probability may see you as a threat, and that can be career ending. Be aware of your situation and adjust accordingly.

If your managers and/or supervisors are not actually involved in your success, it may be time to survey the marketplace or landscape for a new opportunity or start your own enterprise. Don't get to retirement age and say, "If I had only …" or "What was I thinking?"

What might of, could of or should of have been doesn't mean much when you're sixty-five or seventy. You thought life was tough before, when you didn't have time to do anything to improve and reap the benefits. What do you think it will be when you run out of time and have nothing to offer?

Being an adult and professional is the direct opposite of going along to get along. Just remember, Leaders always have goals and objectives, lead from the front, and expect the best and not after the fact. Fundamentally, people follow leadership not titles.

OBSERVATION

Here are some thoughts on goal setting:

1. Are your goals and objectives *realistic*?

2. Are your goals and objectives *relative* and *time bound*?

3. Are your goals and objectives *measurable*?

4. Are your goals and objectives *written down*?

5. Are your goals and objectives *agreed to by all parties involved*?

You don't become a world champion by becoming the best you can be. You become a world champion by becoming the best of the rest.

You don't become an Olympic champion by training three times a week. You become an Olympic champion by training every day for 1,460 days (four years).

You don't become a US Navy SEAL because you can run, swim, and do a lot of push-ups. You become a US Navy SEAL because you want to and/or are willing to run, swim, and do more push-ups than the next guy even when you are cold, wet, tired, and hungry. The US Navy SEALs are interested only in those who truly understand that teamwork and the mission are more important than how they feel.

> No matter what your pursuit, never quit on yourself or your dreams!

INSIGHT 13

To begin each day knowing war *in business means ... We are ready!*

To me, everything is a project and every project has a beginning and an end.

Pretty simple.

Project management provides the platform to anticipate and/or alleviate most of the problems if addressed properly during the planning process. The only unknowns are, well, the unknowns. You know the surprises—for example, weather, delivery, and the education and training of staff. And yes, there are plenty of other unknowns for you to contemplate.

I have been fortunate to assist companies in building and relocating their manufacturing facilities and to direct their ISO certification efforts using the principles of project management. As part of those adventures, I also considered contingency plans, such as checklists, risk assessments, or simulations, if warranted. You know the what-if part. If you don't consider them up front, you probably will be invited to participate in their resolution the hard way.

One of the key components of project management is team building, but I think that may be overused and emphasized for the wrong reasons. In my opinion, team building has replaced critical thinking. Today, its politically correct group think. You know, "We don't want to offend anyone." However, to achieve success each member of the team must perform at the highest level for the team to be effective. That means you have to be an adult, professional, and respectful at all times. In the decision-making process, no one ever leads from the front through consensus. Indecision produces inactions, delays, or non-resolutions to the problems, issues, questions, or concerns at hand.

Get the facts. Consider any ramifications and make the decision today!

OBSERVATION

This is my definition of a team:

> The downfall of a team member is
> the downfall of the team.

If you know that a team member is having difficulties and needs assistance and you fail to recognize it and/or ignore it, I believe the problem may be you, not the individual team member. If you know of the problem, issue, question, or concern, or if you can assist in its resolution but decide its sink-or-swim time, it's you who is the liability to the team.

Allowing people to fail as a learning tool may be acceptable under controlled conditions, but it must be implemented correctly, i.e., legally, morally, and ethically. Besides, you need to keep the front doors open during your education and training initiatives. However, allowing a project, program, or team member to fail is not leadership; it's protectionism and totally unacceptable.

You should encourage opinions, options, and recognize obstacles and difficulties, but at the end of the day, as the leader, you must make the decision. Decision by committee is acquiescence of your authority and position. Get the information you need to make the decision and then move on to the next task or problem.

Never misunderstand confrontational dialogue as non-commitment, while understanding that the absence of dialog is communication without sound.

> As I said to my son one time,
> the older you get, the smarter I am.

EPILOGUE

Is America Looking Beyond the Obvious?

First I think we need to look at what, if anything has changed in America. Let's see if these twenty-five insights parallel or overlap the changes in the America we live in today. My intention here is not to lecture or present a dissertation on how this happened or why it happened. We all know it has happened and continues to happen because we are living with the implications of change every day.

America now seems to frown on ingenuity, technology, and good old-fashioned hard work. America has gone from entrepreneurship to complacency. In the past fifty or sixty years, the American economy has gone from predominance to dependence. Government's economic theories, rules, and regulations that have advocated spending, spending, and more spending have systematically priced this country out of business and, along with taxes, have incrementally chipped away at the foundations of our very freedom. I am not opposed to government and taxes; I'm opposed to unnecessary and expensive government which is being paid for by more and more taxes from the less and less gainfully employed people.

Under the umbrella of the global economy or whatever is being served up as today's special, the American people have allowed themselves to accept social programs without fully understanding the long-range implications or consequences. We could have saved trillions of dollars by just looking at yesterday, evaluating our history, and looking beyond the obvious.

Bumper-sticker philosophies; politicians' insatiable drive to resolve all our problems, questions, issues, and concerns at our expense; and their reassuring speeches have replaced critical thinking. Good intentions have grown our national debt so it's no longer money we owe ourselves but money we don't have and we'll never see.

Politicians always talk about cutting taxes or about programs being underfunded or cut. In government speak; a reduction in the budget request is a cut. Here's how it works: You request a 15 percent increase in your budget. After some smoke and mirrors, the committee proudly announces that it settled on 8 percent, thus saving the taxpayer 7 percent. The savings of course are imaginary, and the taxpayer is again on the hook for an additional 8 percent increase. So grows the budget!

Hey, wait a minute. Did your last salary increase match that? I seriously doubt it. As a result, all public and private costs now rise, and you get to pay the bill again. So convince yourself again why these problems remaining unsolved are a good thing.

Am I supposed to believe that the rich are simply not paying enough taxes? Even if that were true, what happens when the rich just stop investing? Do you tax what's remaining in after-tax funds also? You already do! Ever hear of savings accounts, estate taxes, and capital gains, to name a few?

Now what?

One side screams, "We can't live with these cuts," while the other side proudly boasts that it is working for the middle class—"Look how I'm looking out for you." Multiply that mind-set by how many government budgets we are supposedly saving money on, and you quickly get the picture of our national debt. As they say, "That's the facts, Jack."

I am only pointing out that we have spent all our money, and with taxes always rising, it's hard not to see why we are in debt. We now owe our financial well-being and our very existence to foreign investors, both the good and bad guys. How can we control our own destiny if we have no money? Keep printing more? And how will that help?

The problem is quite simple. "We the People" of the United States have not fully acknowledged there even is a problem. Until that happens, we will continue to have historical illusions of future greatness, gifted debates as to who is at fault, and one-sided solutions.

Is that what you want? To continue down the same path expecting a different destination? What can we do to change this? Please consider these insights:

1. Look beyond the obvious.

    Question everything, propose viable alternatives, and make your position known.

    Don't accept what someone else thinks is best for you and your family. That's your responsibility and your decision. Make it!

    Get the facts. Get involved. Make a difference!

    Who is in charge of ME, Inc.? You or someone else?

2. We need leaders, not managers, and certainly not career politicians.

    Why do we keep electing the same people or the same ideology to public office and expect a different result? Is that what this "hope and change" smoke-and-mirrors shell game is all about? It's a delusionary illusion.

    Being an elected official is a privilege not a career. These people believe they are above the law because they write the law, and of course they are not subject to its provisions. Term limits solve this mirage in a heartbeat.

3. We need to teach the next generation why American is relevant, important, successful, and exceptional. I've always

found it fascinating that we continue to have the richest poor in the world.

Remember, it wasn't the citizens of the United States who created this mess. It was those enlightened among us who are so concerned about our well-being, our education, the climate, the poor, and special interests that spend an inordinate amount of their time plotting against those evil rich people. And we, the citizens of the United States have collectively bought into their cleverly designed and packaged false arguments about programs and policies.

Coupled with the constant drone of negativity from the politically correct, who are trying to save us from ourselves at our own expense, and the guiding light of our incorruptible politicians, it's truly amazing we have survived this long as a country.

It gets to the point where the squeaky wheel now constitutes consensus. This deafening roar eventually drowns out any reasonable debate. When everyone is yelling and screaming is it any wonder that no one can actually hear? I am not sure how you can listen when you can't hear yourself think.

Thanks to these self-appointed guardians of our lives, those wonderful, insightful, compassionate ideas are now the policy, rules, and regulations we live under. They are controlling our lives evermore, and now we are paying the price for it dearly.

When is enough … enough?

4. We need citizens and entrepreneurs who believe in ingenuity, labor-saving technology, and the hard work to make it happen, not rules and regulations for the sake of rules and regulations. Over seventy-five-thousand-plus pages of tax code?

This is helping how?

How many businesses can you point to that were started because of the tax codes? Probably not many. I would bet not as many as those started in spite of the tax codes though.

For those who believe that redistribution of wealth always works, they are absolutely 100 percent correct. It always works with other people's money until you run out of money as Margret Thatcher once reasoned.

We need citizens who believe in liberty and freedom, but not at the expense of others'. When we have entrepreneurship, liberty, and freedom, the result is magical.

5. We need an informed and vigilant public that understands and believes freedom is not and never will be negotiable, nor is it free. It takes time, money, commitment, and sometimes treasure to preserve, and sometimes it costs dearly.

6. We need citizens who understand why the US Constitution is not a "living document" and that its sole purpose is to protect the citizens of the United States from the government of the United States and not the government of the United States from the citizens of the United States. If the rules are constantly changing, you have in essence no rules at all, and therefore you have no freedom.

7. There is a simple correlation between the size of government and the US economy. The more government, the more cost to the economy. The more cost to the economy, the more difficult to get ahead. The more difficult to get ahead, the less people try. The less people try, the slower the economy grows and more people ultimately become dependent on the government. The more people who become dependent, the more government needs to raise taxes (taxes cloaked in clever, enterprising words like *investment* and *fees*) to support the ever-increasing population that quits trying and/or demands assistance. The more people who quit trying and/or demand assistance, the more government expands. The more government expands, the more it costs. And so it goes.

   Why? The problem is actually quite simple.

   Apparently you don't know how to allocate your money for your own benefit because you allowed elected or unelected bureaucrats to perform this service for you. The citizens of the United States keep approving this nonsense, so the government keeps taxing and spending. This cycle only continues at the indulgence of the US citizens.

In your lifetime have your expenses and taxes actually ever gone down? Of course not. Can you honestly say you are living a less-restrictive lifestyle today than when you were growing up? Probably not.

Take the blinders off and open your eyes. Take a hard look around! Are you any safer in Chicago, Los Angles, or Detroit today than yesterday? Are you more economically well off than your parents? And you think your liberties and freedoms haven't been affected?

Why are you still working until spring of each year just to pay your taxes if they have gone down? If you are not a business owner, did you know that you are only paying for one half of your Social Security tax because your employer pays the other half?

Have you ever seen this tax go down? I'll guarantee your employer hasn't.

Some people say we have more people with more needs. Although there is some truth in that assessment, I think we can pay for a lot of needs with $18 trillion, don't you?

Think about this: If you had $18 trillion and divided it by 20 million people in need, you would have $900,000 per person. Would that get you out of poverty and kick-start your life? Maybe, but you would be hard-pressed to convince me that continuing down our current path of spending more and more money will result in a different outcome than what we have been experiencing.

Do you think we might be able to solve our problems for less? Has that question ever been seriously addressed in the past fifty years? If money was the solution, just give me the number, add 20 percent for a buffer, and solve the problem.

Too simplistic? Convince me otherwise!

Why do we still have this war on poverty? The answer is always "If we just had more time and more money we could solve this problem." These programs have been funded by you and me for fifty years. Fifty years! Is that enough time?

Common sense dictates this noble cause is only mathematically able to sustain itself because the American public is accepting the premise that it is morally correct even if there is no end in sight to resolving the problem. There may be no end in sight, but there is also no money in sight at the end of the tunnel either.

Only our technology has offset the massive costs of these programs. But what happens when our technology stagnates? Owners, CEOs, and company presidents have all told me it is virtually impossible to hire people with any concept of work and those who do get hired don't want to work anyway.

We aren't graduating engineers and scientists; we are graduating functional illiterates. Sound harsh? You may disagree, but you probably haven't talked with enough business owners and CEOs lately. Will the new technologies come from graduates who can't even read and write at the high school level?

As a country, if we don't reinvest in manufacturing, invent new technologies, create jobs in the private sector, and continue to support our economy, we can't support those ever-increasing program costs. Then what?

OBSERVATION

Do you realize that some people think $200 billion is more than $1 trillion because two hundred is greater than one?

No, I'm not kidding!

A trillion dollars is a term we just don't use every day. It's hard to visualize or conceptualize, and we have never had to deal with numbers of that magnitude. Check this out: it takes twelve steps to get from one dollar to $1 trillion when multiplying by a factor of ten.

$$$	X	Multiplier	=	Total $$$
1	X	10	=	10
10	X	10	=	100
100	X	10	=	1,000
1,000	X	10	=	10,000
10,000	X	10	=	100,000
100,000	X	10	=	1,000,000
1,000,000	X	10	=	10,000,000
10,000,000	X	10	=	100,000,000
100,000,000	X	10	=	1,000,000,000
1,000,000,000	X	10	=	10,000,000,000
10,000,000,000	X	10	=	100,000,000,000
100,000,000,000	X	10	=	1,000,000,000,000

Translated, it takes one thousand billions to equal one trillion. That's a lot of money, no matter how you calculate it, and the United States is eighteen times over that in debt!

Here's another way to look at this: A sports figure makes $40 million per year. How many years would it take for that sports figure to earn $1 trillion?

A. 2.5 years

B. 10 years

C. 25 years

D. 38.5 years

E. Over 50 years

$1,000,000,000,000 ÷ $40,000,000/year = 25,000 years

And yes, that is correct!

Why do we allow this insanity to continue? Indifference, apathy, or just plain whatever? In reality, the answer totally depends on you.

You need to ask yourself the following five questions:

1. What do you really want for yourself and family? Why? (What is the purpose of your goal?)

2. When do you really want to achieve it? (What's your time frame?)

3. How are you going to get it? (What's your game plan?)

4. Who is standing up for you, your family, your business and America? (ME, Inc.)

5. If not you, who? If not now, when?

The answers will impact you, your family, your business and America for generations.

So here's the bottom line for you and your business:

SEVEN RULES FOR BUSINESS SUCCESS

1. Leaders lead from the front and not from the office.

2. Ensure that your employees, customers, bankers, insurance agents and companies, accountants, financial and legal services, suppliers, and stakeholders understand the dynamics of revenue, growth, and profitability.

3. Ensure your employees truly embrace change.

4. Ensure you continue to innovate with products and services that

    - Nobody thought of or knows about (innovation),
    - Everyone needs (creates the desire to take action), and
    - Can't get anywhere else (that's what makes you unique).

5. Ensure that your employees, customers, bankers, insurance agents and companies, accountants, financial and legal services,

suppliers, and stakeholders become your business partners to make things happen *for* you ... not *to* you.

6. Ensure your community recognizes good corporate neighbors.

7. Ensure that you look beyond the obvious in all things.

NOTES

NOTES

NOTES

www.ingramcontent.com/pod-product-compliance
Lightning Source LLC
Chambersburg PA
CBHW021944170526
45157CB00003B/922